The Chapels

In the Western Isles

Finlay MacLeod

illustrations
by Christine Campbell

acair

First published in Scotland in 1997 by Acair Ltd., 7 James Street, Stornoway, Isle of Lewis.

This text was published initially in Gaelic by Acair Limited for SRG in 1997, and subsequently translated into English by Acair Limited for this publication.

Printed by Stornoway Gazette, Stornoway, Isle of Lewis.

ISBN 0 86152 108 0

Contents

Starting-off.

This book aims to be a guide for those who are out and about in the Western Isles and who are seeking to find out more about the many interesting features here — in this case the range of chapel sites situated throughout the Islands. The location of the sites is given and reference is made to the writings of earlier visitors to the sites.

The book does not aim to provide a detailed description of the buildings but is intended more as an introductory text to encourage younger people to take an active interest in the Hebridean environment and culture. The book was published earlier in Gaelic as a text for secondary school students. It could just as easily be a book about Island wells, stills, corn mills, kilns, early schools, etc: the particular topic serves mainly to encourage people to go out into the countryside to enjoy its varied texture.

For those wishing to go on to learn more about the historical framework within which the chapels may be placed they could begin with the writings of Ian B. Cowan and particularly his book, 'The Parishes of Medieval Scotland' (1967), and his seminal paper, 'The Development of the Parochial System in Medieval Scotland'. Cowan writes that the basic unit in the organisation of the Medieval Church in Scotland was the parish. The pattern of parishes established by the twelfth century lasted until the Reformation. The chapels of the Western Isles are described in the present book according to the various parishes within the diocese which was named 'Sodor'.

On the ground, one imagines the visitor or student in the vicinity of one of the sites, and being approached by a local resident who is working on his croft on the machair:

"That is Teampall Eòin ahead of you," ventures the crofter. "St. John's Chapel."

"I thought it was," says the seeker, writing the name in his notebook.

He writes: "Teampall Eòin. St. John's Chapel. NB 288488".

"It is also called Cill Sgàire," ventures the crofter.

"How very unusual," the visitor.

"Very unusual," the crofter. "Viking influence."

The crofter turns round and points: "There used to be a special well along there. Called Fuaran Buaile Dhòmhnaill. But it was destroyed by a digger a few years ago."

"The Well on Donald's Enclosure?" translates the visitor.

"The Well on Donald's Enclosure," reassures the crofter.

"Maybe it was used by the priests from the Chapel."

"How old is the Chapel?" asks the visitor.

The crofter laughs. "No idea, No idea whatsoever. Only the ruined site and its name remain."

"Surprising, that," observes the visitor.

"Surprising, indeed," muses the crofter.

The names of most of the chapels have survived and they too are included in this book. In a few instances the actual site cannot be located accurately although the name survives. St. Clement's in Ness in Lewis is one such example. The names reflect the changes that occurred within the early Church in the Gaelic areas; the earlier phase of naming is seen in the chapels dedicated to Saints such as Ronan, Donan, Moluidh and Columba, and the later influences of the centralist Church is seen in names such as St. Peter's, St. John's and St. Mary's. These names are frequently used for the burial grounds where chapels are located, as well as for nearby physical features such as streams or hills, and also for wells which are sometimes found close to the chapels.

Tradition has retained scant knowledge of the priests who attended the chapels or how the chapels themselves were integrated into the everyday communities of the times. The chapels tend to be fairly small and are situated usually near the shore, where the older townships were located. It is intriguing to observe where each of the many sites is located throughout the Islands: it is sometimes as puzzling to understand why there isn't a site in a given township as it is to understand why others are situated where they are.

In terms of access, it is easier to walk round these sites in winter or early in spring when they are clear of nettles and other growth. Not infrequently the sites are in old and sometimes abandoned burial grounds and very few of them have been cared for in any way. Most of them are fairly dilapidated and only a small number have been renovated.

In a way, it is surprising how the chapels have survived, unattended but undamaged during the Islands' numerous church vicissitudes. But they survive in silence; with little interest in them and little done to bring them to the attention of the Islands' young or to revive them in any form of art or festival.

One's quest could readily begin with the site nearest to home.

You will note whether or not it is set in an old burial-ground.

You will note whether or not it is close to an old, pre-crofting settlement.

You will note whether or not there is a special, named well nearby.

There may be someone living in the village who will know something about the site, including its name or any related tradition.

Each Local History Society is likely to have some basic information about the sites in the locality.

The local library will direct you to some books which include accounts written by visitors in earlier years.

The archaeological work on the chapel sites has been very patchy and little progress has been made since the comprehensive 1928 ancient monuments survey. Most of the buildings are beautifully small, in rectangular form. Some of the smaller ones have a nave and chancel but these are few and far between. In many cases the sites have become seriously denuded with only the base outline of the walls remaining; in some cases only a green knoll marks the site. The buildings that have been renovated most extensively include Tùr Mòr Chiamain/St. Clement's, Rodil, Teampall Mholuidh, Ness, the church on Ensay, and Cille Bharra in Barra. The largest of the ruined sites are at Howmore in South Uist, Carinish in North Uist, and Eye in Lewis.

These largely abandoned sites together build up a most intriguing network of locations throughout the length of the Western Isles; the fact that they still exist is surprising in itself, and the fact that they form such an unspoken part of the landscape and the history of the place contrasts with the more strident forms of belief which arrived in the Islands during subsequent centuries.

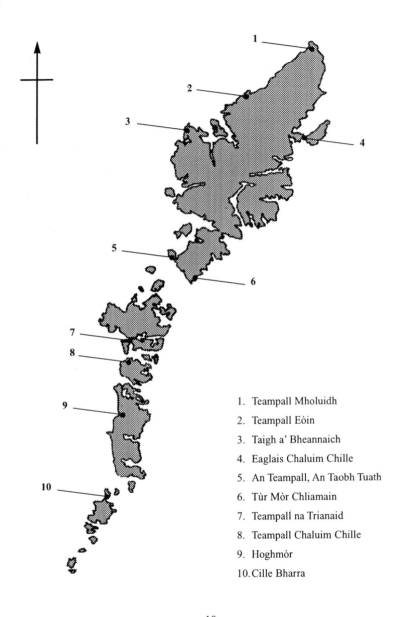

1. Teampall Mholuidh
2. Teampall Eòin
3. Taigh a' Bheannaich
4. Eaglais Chaluim Chille
5. An Teampall, An Taobh Tuath
6. Tùr Mòr Chliamain
7. Teampall na Trianaid
8. Teampall Chaluim Chille
9. Hoghmòr
10. Cille Bharra

Lewis

1. Teampall Rònain

NB 524654

This site is located on a hillock approximately a mile south-east of the Butt of Lewis lighthouse. It is among the Eoropie crofts, and only the foundations remain. It was originally about 24 feet long and 18 feet wide. There is no evidence of a graveyard close to it. Hardly anyone visits this site now although it is quite accessible.

Folklore relates that this chapel was associated with St. Ronan and the story is told of how he left Eoropie and how he got to North Rona on the back of a large whale. (See *Carmina Gadelica*, 1, 1972, 126-7; Robson, 1991, 2-6 and 165).

St. Ronan's Well is by the main road, but when the road was widened the well was badly affected. Often chapels and wells were located close to one another.

Teampall Mholuidh

2. *Teampall Mholuidh*

This is a famous chapel and you can see why.

It is old and imposing and a lot has been written and told about it. It is located in Eoropie and many people visit it because it is accessible to the main road by a footpath.

According to historians such as W.C. Mackenzie it was once called 'Teampall Mòr' by the inhabitants. There is no sign of a graveyard close by although there may well have been one.

It is almost 45 feet long and 18 feet wide with tall limestone walls and attractive windows. To the north a small room is attached and a little chapel is similarly attached to the south side. It was re-roofed in 1912 and it is still used for worship. The chapel features highly in oral tradition as follows:

• how the people knelt as soon as they could see the chapel, although they may be miles away from it.

• how they believed that a person suffering from mental illness could be restored to health by sleeping there for one night, tied to the alter.

• how they walked clockwise round it.

• how they placed a piece of wood in similar shape to the affected part of the body (i.e. hand or foot) to enable actual healing to take place.

• how they used water from St. Ronan's Well nearby.

• how they held their Halloween feasts there before going

out to eat and dance and offer a cup of ale to the god
Seònaidh on a nearby beach. (See Martin, 1934, 107-108;
Pochin Mould, 1953, 175-178).

3. Teampall Thòmais NB 507641

All that remains on this site is a few stones from one of the
walls. It is at the top of a grassy hill by the shore on
Swainbost machair, and there is a hollow within the site. It
is approximately 100 yards from St. Peter's Chapel and
there is no sign of gravestones in close proximity.
According to tradition its stones were used to build St.
Peter's.

4. *Teampall Pheadair* NB 508637

This site is located in the old graveyard in Swainbost and is the second largest chapel in Lewis. The largest is St. Columba's at Eye.

St. Peter's is over 60 feet long, but the only remaining part is the southernmost end which has an attractive window.

It is in a beautiful location, in the western spot of the graveyard with the Swainbost river close by.

Between it and the shore is a place called 'Na h-Annaidean' and 'Cnoc an Annaid'. 'Annaid' is an ancient name for a church location. This name also is found in Shader, close to St. Peter's Chapel, and on Killegray in the Sound of Harris, and in Eilean Garbh on the Shiants.

5. *Teampall Chliamain* NB 4962

Located in North Dell, there is no sign of this site now, nor much account of it in oral tradition. Martin Martin calls it, 'St. Clemen in Dell'.

The Ordnance Survey Book (ONB) writes, "Dun Cleamon... It's site is now ploughed over. A polished stone was found near site of dun (1890). Site is not known locally."

6. *Teampall nan Crò Naomh* NB 433593

This chapel is on South Galson machair, down by the shore. Martin Martin refers to it as 'Holy-Cross church in Galan'.

It is important because Daniel made a painting of it in 1819 when it was mainly intact although without a roof. The gables have since collapsed and sand covers much of the site.

There are three windows in the east wall and there are holes in the inside of the walls.

According to tradition it was once thatched with heather.

7. *Teampall Bhrìghid* NB 410573

This chapel is situated in Melbost; with a few gravestones round about it. All that remains is the raised site and a few stones. Many of the stones have been removed, or have disappeared into the ground.

St. Brighid's Well is close by.

According to tradition, Swain, a Norse king is buried here with his crown and his sword.

8. *Teampall Pheadair* NB 379550

This chapel is situated on a green sward above Mol Eire in Shader. A grassy knoll can still be seen on the site with a small amount of wall still showing. It was over 33 feet long and apparently it comprised two rooms; these were the nave and chancel.

Beside the chapel is Creag Gille Phàdraig. Clach an t-Sagairt could at one time be seen by the shore until it was eroded by the force of the sea some years back.

St. Andrew's Well, mentioned by Martin Martin, can be found east of the chapel, and Tobair Mhoire is slightly to the south of it.

Rubha na h-Annaid lies 100 yards east of the chapel and the large stones which are called Clachan na h-Annaid are about 100 yards south of Rubha na h-Annaid near St. Andrew's Well.

9. *Teampall Mhoire*

This chapel was situated in Barvas cemetery but it is now engulfed by sand.

We know that it was there in the 15th century because a letter from the Pope in Rome dated 27 May, 1403, states, "To all the Christian faithful — Indult granting an indulgence to visitors to the church of St. Mary in Barwas in the isle of Lewis, diocese of Sodor, on certain feast days and those who contribute to its reparation", as if people could not normally use it, and it also suggests that it was even then being repaired.

According to Dean Monro (1549) this chapel was one of 4 parish churches in Lewis: the others were in Ness, in Uig and in Point (Cowan, 1967).

In his book, A Tour of the Hebrides (1803) James Hogg writes "On the top of one of these hills is situated St. Mary's chapel, an ancient place of Popish worship. It had formerly been on the very summit of the eminence, but the sand is now heaped up to such a height as to be on a level with the gables. Yet the eddying winds have still kept it nearly clear, so that it appears as a building wholly sunk underground. The baptismal font is still standing in a place in the wall prepared for it." (III).

In 1861 T.S. Muir wrote, "The church — St. Mary — is said to be existing under the sand, which has also completely overwhelmed the ancient graveyard." (186).

10. Teampall Eòin

NB 288488

This chapel is known by two names: St. John's Chapel and Cill Sgàire. 'Cill' is Celtic, and Sgàire is a personal Norse name still found in Lewis: St. John's Chapel is the newer and more Roman name.

This is an attractive building and it is better preserved than many other chapels. It can be found in the old Bragar graveyard.

It is approximately 29 feet long and has two rooms; the nave and chancel. Experts are of the opinion that it was built in the 15th century.

At one time there was a special spring close by called Fuaran Buaile Dhòmhnaill but a JCB destroyed it some years back. The remains of an old village can be seen adjacent to the graveyard and a kitchen midden can be seen above the shore line. An underground channel was discovered between that spot and the graveyard itself a few years back.

Teampall Eòin

11. *Teampall Dail Mòr* NB 218448

This building was knocked down sometime after 1914 and the stones were used to build the house next door. T.S. Muir wrote in 1885, "At Dailmor... the remains of an apparently not very old chapel, 60 feet in length." (41-2). In the Royal Commission (1928) it is written that they visited it in 1914: "This church... is of comparatively recent date. It is an ordinary oblong structure with no features of interest." (1).

There is no sign of it nowadays and even its name is unknown. There was no graveyard near it. Martin Martin does not mention it; maybe it had not been built when he visited.

Between the two wars visitors came to seek it out, but the man next door told them, "Gone... Gone..." Gone indeed.

12. *Teampall Chiarain* NB 187424

This chapel was situated in Carloway, above Laimsiadair, but cannot now be seen. Historic references tell us that those who were ill were brought to this chapel and that they were walked clockwise round the building, and made to sleep the night inside. They believed that this would cure the afflicted person.

Close by was a cairn at the top of a steep path, called 'Slighe Chiarain'; the cairn was known as 'Beannachadh Ciaraig' (NB 190424). Passers by would place a stone on the cairn; the site can still be seen.

At the end of Slighe Chiarain and slightly to the north is Fuaran Chiarain. Martin Martin mentions this spring and says that water from it could not successfully wash linen.

13. *Teampall Mhìcheil*   NB 195417

This chapel was in Kirvick in Carloway but only the base foundation exists today. It is in an old cemetery.

T.S. Muir wrote in 1861, "Hardly anything of it remains, and the burying-ground is now but rarely used." (186). The Ordnance Survey map of 1850 refers to the village beside the graveyard as 'Baile an Teampaill'.

14. *Teampall Dhonain*   NB 152406

This site can be found at the south end of Tràigh an Teampaill in Little Bernera. It is also called the Teampall Iosal. Only the shape remains, covered in grass and sand. Close by are Rubha Phapanais and Cnoc an t-Sagairt.

In 1861 T.S. Muir wrote, "Another chapel — St. Donnan — was standing not many years since lower down on a snout of land close to the beach, but no traces of it are now extant." (177).

The lovely tale is told of Swain the Norse king, and how he took Gealchos, daughter of the young priest with him from Tràigh an Teampaill to Norway. But her heart broke mourning for Little Bernera and he brought her back. Her song is still known. (see D. Dòmhnallach, 1967, 228-234).

15. *Teampall Mhìcheil* NB 151406

This site is also on Little Bernera, and nothing is left save the rise of the walls. It is beside the burial aisle of John Macdonald which is built similar to an old chapel.

T.S. Muir writes in 1861, "Directly above a smaller tràigh (Tràigh an Teampaill) on the eastern side of the island, there is an open burying-ground, containing a few bare slabs of ancient type, and the groundwork of St. Michael's chapel occupying the top of a rock." (177). Muir stayed with John Macdonald at Taigh a' Chaolais at the time.

A short distance from Little Bernera is Eilean Fir Chrothair (NB 139418) which has stone beehive dwellings, with one of them still almost intact. The local people call it 'Am Beannachadh' (The Blessing Place). Small buildings similar to these can be seen on remote islands in different places throughout the islands; they could have been prayer houses used by anchorites.

16. *Teampall Chirceboist* NB 191346

In the village of Kirkibost in Bernera can be found the site of an old chapel. Locals believe that this is the chapel referred to in Martin Martin's book as 'St. Macrel'. Origines (1857) refers to it as 'Saint Macra the Virgin'.

An old graveyard is close to the chapel and another site called, 'An Taigh Sgoile'. The chapel site is near Loch Mharcoil, and maybe it was called 'Teampall Mharcoil'.

Macaulay (c 1984) says that there is a Teampall Chaluim Chille in Great Bernera, but if there is, no-one knows where.

17. *Teampall Pheadair* NB 105376

Situated on the lovely island of Pabbay close to Valtos, Uig, and above Tràigh na Cille, this chapel has all but disappeared. The lower walls remain, with the sill of one window to the west. It looks as if a chancel was situated at the east end.

"The church on Pabay More in Loch Roag, Lewis, bears a dedication to St. Peter. This marks the grafting of the new style on the old. After the synod of Whitby (664) the Celtic Church gradually conformed to Roman usages, including that of dedications. How soon or how late this change would affect the Isles is impossible to say." (Royal Commission, 1928, xlvii).

T.S. Muir wrote in 1861, "Made up of smooth sandy beach, rock, and flowery pasture, Eilean Pabba had much of that peculiar sweetness of aspect which somehow invariably belongs to islands of the name... The scant remains of St. Peter's chapel — a rude and narrow oblong some eight-and-twenty feet in length in the middle of a nearly obliterated burying-ground — being the only object of interest." (177).

Two interesting lobster ponds can be found at the north end of the island.

18. Teampall Bhaltois   NB 089367

This chapel is in the Valtos graveyard above Cliff Beach.

T.S. Muir writes in 1885, "... the foundations of a chapel, internally 18 feet in length." (41). Its name is unknown. To this day a knoll in the graveyard is referred to as 'An Teampall', and the surrounding area is called 'Leathad an Teampaill'.

A raised grassy spot about a mile south-east of this site is called 'An Teampall' (NB 098363). It is close to the northwest end of Tràigh na Beirghe.

Taigh a' Bheannaich

19. *Taigh a' Bheannaich* NB 038378

About a mile south west of Gallan Head in Uig this site is close to the shore, and to a headland called 'Am Beannachadh' (The Blessing Place), close to Loch a' Bheannaich. Tobair a' Bheannaich is about 32 yards south west of the chapel.

D. Macdonald (1967) also mentions, 'Geò a' Bheannaich' and 'Faing a' Bheannaich'.

T.S. Muir writing in 1861 says, "On Gallon Head — Tigh Beannaichte (Blessed House), or Tigh Beannachadh (Blessing House), as it is locally called — is, except that the roof is wanting, nearly entire. The internal dimensions are 18ft. 2in., by 10ft. 4in. From the appearance of the masonry, which is without lime, and other peculiar features, it would seem a very old building." (174).

20. An Teampall, Baile na Cille   NB 048339

This chapel was situated in the graveyard at Baile na Cille, and is referred to by Martin Martin as 'St. Christopher's'. The writer I.N. MacLeòid was of the opinion that it was called Cille Chrìosd.

The Royal Commission (1928) says, "There is an old kirkyard, beside the highest part of which stood an old church built in 1724. The site was occupied by an earlier church, Capail Mor ("Big Chapel"), the foundations of which are said to be traceable in spring. To the south of it is the site of Capail Beg ("Little Chapel"), possibly a still earlier church." (18).

It is strange that oral tradition does not provide more information on these chapels. Maybe this is as a consequence of the fact that chapels were being built and knocked down round about Baile na Cille.

21. Teampall, Mealasta   NB 990243

Mealista is the most westerly village in Uig.

T.S. Muir states in 1885, "At Mealastadh, on its south-west side, are traces of a small building called Taigh nan Cailleachan Dubha, House of the Black Old Women (Nuns); and in an open, grassy, and flowery burial-ground, the foundations of a chapel, internally about 19 feet in length, and a rudely-formed font of elleptical shape." (40).

And the Royal Commission (1928) says, "About 200 yards west of Mealista farmhouse, on a rocky point on the south of the promontary Rudh' an Teampaill, rising only 20 feet above high water mark, are the foundations of the church, measuring externally 25 feet in length and 15 feet 8 inches in breadth, with the wall 2 feet 8 inches thick and oriented south of east and north of west. Between the church and the sea is a small burying ground. (18).

"At Mealista, Uig, there was a shrine to St Catan (see Teampall na h-Aoidh), near which has been found the remains of a nunnery, locally known as the 'house of the black old women'." (W.C. Mackenzie, 1903, 518).

Strangely there is no reference in oral tradition to Taigh nan Cailleachan Dubha — only the name and location. In Lewis one often spoke of the distance along the west coast by saying, "From the House of the Black Women in Uig to Taigh Mholuidh in Eoropie."

22. *Teampall Chaluim Chille*   NB 386211

St Columba's Isle in Loch Erisort is well known in Lewis history as a fertile, beautiful and peaceful spot. St. Columba's chapel is situated in the graveyard on that island.

"The church is oblong on plan and measures internally 29 feet 6 inches by 13 feet 3 inches, the walls still standing to an average of 6 feet and measuring 2 feet 6 inches thick." (Royal Commission, 1928, 11).

One of Derick Thomson's poems bemoans how the place has changed: 'Eilean Chaluim Chille, an Loch Eireasort, Leòdhas' (1967).

23. An Teampall, Rànais   NB 399248

There is a site in Ranish called Cnoc an Teampaill where the remains of an old graveyard are still evident and the lower part of the chapel walls.

It was approximately 20 feet long by 12 feet wide. Nowadays no-one can tell of its history although the name of the area is still used. We have no knowledge of the name of the chapel.

24. An Teampall, Cathanais   NB 389234

Martin Martin refers to this chapel as St. Pharaer in Kaeness. Cathanais is located in Suardail in Loch Liurbost, but the remains of the chapel is no longer visible. At one time there was a farm and a township here. Neither is it known who St. Pharaer was, and there is no reference to such a saint anywhere else. Martin Martin did not elaborate, but merely referred to him as St. Pharaer in Kaeness. Some do not accept that this was the chapel to which Martin referred; and that he might really have meant the Ranish chapel.

25. *Teampall Leannain*

This chapel was situated in central Stornoway, although all that now remains is the name and the church bell. Martin Martin referred to it as 'St. Lennan in Sternvay'. It was situated in a graveyard on North Beach close to where the Royal Bank of Scotland and the Sailors' Home are at present. One of the chapel doors was later used as the outside door of a shoemaker's shop in the town. W.C. Mackenzie (1919) states, "St Lennan was built by the 1st Earl of Seaforth who died in 1633 — the pre-Reformation church having fallen into disrepair."

Macaulay (c1984) says, "The pre-Reformation church at Stornoway was dedicated to St. Adamnan." (42). But he does not disclose the source of his information.

An account written by Lord Teignmouth in 1829 tells of how the tide was intruding into the graveyard and exposing the remains. It is also related that the building was in danger of falling and that it was one, Dòmhnall Ceàrd who eventually demolished it for the reward of one and a half bolls of meal. "Oh, Donald Ceàrd of the boll and a half meal. Had you been given the other half you would have had even the Pope's own image on the ground." (D Macdonald, 1967, 297).

The bell from this chapel is still used in St. Peter's in Stornoway.

Martin Martin also mentions 'Stornvay Church' but there is no information available concerning this church.

Eaglais Chaluim Chille

26. *Eaglais Chaluim Chille*

Undoubtedly this church was one of the best known in the islands, and it was the foremost Lewis church at one time. It is situated at Eye and was built by one of the MacLeod chiefs and dedicated to St. Catan. "As Ui was the 'Iona' of Sìol Thorquil, so was Rodil (Tùr Chliamain) the 'Iona' of Sìol Thormod." (W.C. MacKenzie, 1903, 519).

It is a large building but it is neglected and much in need of repair. Each wall and gable is still intact and it is a great pity that no one takes responsibility for it. It is situated in the old Eye Churchyard in Aignish by the shore and many MacLeod chiefs are buried there, and grave slabs can be seen there. Martin Martin refers to it as 'St. Colum in Eye'.

W.C. MacKenzie (1919) states that according to tradition there had been a cell on this site dedicated to St. Catan (6th and 7th century) and a holy house. Much has been written about St. Columba's Church as it is so well known. (see T.S. Muir, 1861, 167; T.S. Muir, 1885, 39-40; Royal Commission, 1928, 12-14; D. Macdonald, 1967, 264-266; Barber, 1987; Bill Lawson, 1991).

27. Teampall Chùistein

This chapel was situated in Garrabost in Point. Martin Martin refers to it as 'St. Cuthcon'. He also says, "The well at St. Cowsten's Church never boils any kind of meat, though it be kept on fire a whole day." (90).

Some think that it was really St. Constantine's, but this may not be so.

T.S. Muir (1861) states, "Of St. Cowstan's chapel, once in Garrabost... nothing now remains, the site having sometime since been ploughed and put under crop; but the holy well, still remembered as that consecrated by the patron saint, and regarded the sweetest water in the place, still trickles down its steep declivity to the shore." (167).

The Ordnance Survey Book (ONB) states the following about the chapel, "It is situated on a piece of sloping ground on the north of and adjacent to Allt Buaile Eòin about 4 chains west of Tobar an Leothaid. Around 1808 the walls were completely levelled for building the walls of huts etc. There is no sign of it today. St. Cowstan's Well: tradition is that all manners of diseases used to be cured by placing the patient under the cliff when the water fell to the shore." (ONB, Lewis, 21, 1848).

28. Teampall Rubha Chirc   NB 507292

Neither Martin Martin nor T.S. Muir refer to this chapel.
But the site is identified on the first Ordnance Survey map
c1850. There is no information about its dedication.

The Royal Commission (1928) says, "About ⅝ mile east
of Chicken Head, in a small enclosure on the left bank of a
small rivulet near the edge of a cliff which rises more than
100 feet out of the sea, are the foundations of a stone and
mud building measuring about 18 feet in length and 15 feet
in breadth, oriented west-north-west and east-south-east."
(14).

29. Teampall Aulaidh   NB 491415

Martin Martin refers to this chapel as 'St. Aula in Grease'.
The Royal Commission (1928) states, "St. Aulay (Olaf) at
Gress, Lewis, is the only Norse saint among the dedications."
(xclvi). (Cill Sgàire is the original name for Teampall Eòin
in Bragar). The walls and gables of this chapel are still
intact, but a shelter has been built at one end of it.

T.S. Muir (1861) states, "Col and Gress, lying some few
miles north of Stornoway, are both sweet spots. At the latter
is the church of St. Aula, standing in an open though
cleanly burying-ground a little way up from the shore: it is
a very small building, the internal length being barely 19

feet, the walls nearly entire, but without any peculiar features." (168).

Above the main door is written '1681 1B MK' — as if it had been repaired that year.

30. Teampall Mhìcheil   NB 544481

This chapel was in North Tolsta, in Cladh Mhìcheil above the Tràigh Mhòr. Martin Martin refers to it as 'St. Michael in Tollasta'.

T.S. Muir (1885) says, "At Tolsta... is the burying-ground of St. Michael, on a grassy slope overlooking a long stretch of smooth sandy shore, but in it are no traces of the church under the dedication mentioned by Martin." (43-44).

Donald Macdonald from Tolsta wrote a book about the village in 1984: "There is now no trace of the old chapel, dedicated to St. Michael, the Celtic Neptune, probably similar to St. Olaf's in Gress, which stood about fifty yards up from the north east corner (of the graveyard), where its large foundation stones can still be found. In 1820 part of its walls were still standing and ponies used to shelter here on cold winter nights." (55).

The stream which runs through the village of Tolsta is called Allt Chaluim Chille.

31. *Teampall Chaluim Chille*

Martin Martin refers to this chapel as 'St. Collum in Garien'.

No one knows of this location. Some people believe it was in Garry.

It is not known whether it had any links with Allt Chaluim Chille in Tolsta.

The Origines (1851) map places it at Cnoc a' Ghearraidh Ghuirm in Coll, but we cannot be certain that this is correct.

32. *Dun Othail and An Luchraban*

(NB 543515)   (NB 511661)

These are two isolated sites and some written accounts refer to them as having been chapels, or prayer houses, as could have been in Eilean Fir Chrothair.

T.S. Muir (1861) states, "At Dun Othail, in a shelf down in the face of the precipice, is an architectural remain — of an early chapel, probably." (168). But there are sites on places such as Dùn Filiscleitir, Dùn Eòradail and Dùn Eistean along this coast, and they have never been referred to as sites of chapels.

Dean Monro (1549) says of the Luchraban, "At the northern poynt of Lewis there is a little ile, callit the

37

Pigmies ile, with ane little kirk in it of ther awn handey wark." (82-83).

An anonymous account written between 1577 and 1599 states, "In this (Pygmies) Isle thair is ane little Cove biggit in form of ane kirk, and callit the Pygmies Kirk." Blaeu's map (1654) also shows it as a chapel and calls the island 'Ylen Dunibeg' (Island of the little people).

Outer Islands

These are Rona and Sulaisgeir; the Shiants; the Flannan Isles; and St. Kilda.

33. Rona   HW 809323

Rona is situated about 50 miles north-east of Ness in Lewis; it is close to Sulasgeir, and they are separated by Caolas Rònaigh — 10 miles wide.

To this day, in Ness, oral tradition relates how St. Ronan fled from Ness to Rona to get peace and quiet, and how he chased the wild things out to sea when he arrived on Rona.

There is a wonderful folktale describing how a huge animal not unlike a whale carried him to Rona on its back. The animal was called a cianaran-crò. (see Carmichael, 1, 126-127; 2, 348; 6, 115-116).

St. Ronan's cell is one of the most important of its kind in Europe. Because the island is so inaccessible the cell walls are still intact. Round about the 12th century a chapel was attached to the cell, and the walls of that chapel can still be seen although they have fallen in part. Writers have related many stories about the Rona people, their customs and their beliefs. It is a most interesting island in every respect. (see Monro, 1549/1961, 88; Martin, 100-104, Morrison (Indweller) c1683/1989, 27; T.S. Muir, 1885, 90-96; Royal Commission, 1928, 3-4; Fraser Darling, 1939; Robson, 1991, 6-9).

There is a collection of stones close to Cill Rònain and maybe this is Teampall Mhionagain, although one cannot be entirely sure. T.S. Muir (1886) mentions that 'Teampall nam Manach' was in this locality.

There were beautiful stone crosses in the graveyard close to the Cell; the most singular one is now with Comann Eachdraidh Nis, as is a round stone dug up by Fraser Darling near the altar in St. Ronan's Cell.

34. Sùlaisgeir

Tradition has it that Rònan's sister — Brianuilt — fled from Rona to Sùlasgeir. There can still be seen there a large stone bench which is called 'Suidhe Bhrianuilt'.

There is also a stone building there like a large beehive dwelling. Unfortunately its roof collapsed a few years ago.

T.S. Muir (1886) states, "On a small semi-insulated spot, closely surrounded by rocks, marked Sgeir an Teampaill in the Ordnance map, there is a low rugged building with rounded corners and curved roof, called Tigh Beanaichte (Blessed House), internally 14 feet long, and 8 feet wide in the middle, and 6 feet 4 inches at the ends." (98).

The Shiants

These islands are about 4 miles east of Park, Lewis. There are three islands: Garbh Eilean; Eilean an Taighe and Eilean Mhuire. They are also known as na h-Eileanan Mòra.

35. Teampall Mhuire NG 431986

Teampall Mhuire was situated on Eilean Mhuire but even the walls are now underground. Apparently it had strong limestone walls, and was situated in the graveyard. Martin Martin says, "Island-More hath a chapel in it dedicated to the Virgin Mary." (105).

36. Eilean Taighe NG 419972

T.S. Muir writing in 1885 said, "On the west side... On this level space there are traces of a burying-ground, and the foundation of what seems to have been a chapel of small size." (56). This is the only known reference to it.

37. Eilean Garbh NG 412983

Airighean na h-Annaid is referred to as a placename on this island. But there is no information about there having been a chapel.

38. The Flannan Isles NB 727469

These islands are 20 miles west of Lewis. They comprise 3 groups of islands, two of which were inhabited: Eilean Mòr and Eilean Taigh. The famous lighthouse and the chapel are situated on Eilean Mòr. This lovely little chapel is still intact. T.S. Muir reports that it was called 'Teampall Beannachadh' (Chapel of Blessing) and there is a spot close to the chapel called 'Am Beannachadh'.

Martin Martin says, "The biggest of these islands is called Island-More; it has the ruins of a chapel dedicated to St. Flannan, from whom the island derives its name. When they (Lewis seabird-hunters) are come to within about 20 paces of the alter, they all strip themselves of their upper garments at once... the first day they say the first prayer, advancing towards the chapel upon their knees; the second prayer is said as they go round the chapel; the third is said hard by or at the chapel." (98).

The Royal Commission (1928) says, "On Eilean Mòr... stand the remains of a tiny chapel. Single chambered and rectangular on plan, it measures only 5 by $7\frac{3}{4}$ feet within walls 26 to 30 inches in thickness. The roof, which had fallen, had been roughly rebuilt. It was built of thin flat slabs... The masonry of the chapel is dry-built and is rude in character, giving no clue to the date of the structure." (30).

39. St. Kilda

Many books have been written about St. Kilda and this trend will probably continue — although no St. Kildans have lived there for 60 years.

Martin Martin says, "There are three chappels on the isle, each of them with one end towards the east, the other towards the west; the alter always placed at the east end; the first of these is called Christ Chappel, near the village; it is covered and thatched after the same manner with their houses... The second of these chappels bears the name of St. Columba, the third of St. Brianan; both built after the manner of Christ's chappel; having churchyards belonging to them, and they are a quarter of a mile distant betwixt each chappel." (443, 445).

In 1764 Macaulay says: "A temple has been dedicated to that illustrious Abbot there, which in the language of the place is called Columbcille to this day: it lies on the west side of the village, and has neither alter, cross or cell within its precincts...

"The largest church on St. Kilda is dedicated to Christ, and is called his temple. It was built of stone, and without any cement: its length is twenty-four feet, and its breadth fourteen. This was in former times the principal place of worship in the isle, and here they continue to bury their dead...

"In St. Kilda, at a distance of a mile from the village, and to the south-west, there is a chapel, in the language of the place called Brendan's temple: It has an alter within, and some Monkish cells without it. These are almost entire and must of consequence be of later date, than the holy places dedicated to Christ and Columba." (69-72).

According to oral tradition there once was a chapel on Boraraigh.

Harris

1. *Teampall Bhrìghid*   NF 007928

This chapel was situated on the site of the present Scarista church, in the old graveyard, in the parish of Kilbride.

T.S. Muir (1885) says, "at Scarista... overlooking along reach of sandy shore, is the modern church of Harris, and close by it the ancient burial-ground in which are a few old-looking gravestones, but no traces of the church which stood there, dedicated to St. Bridget." (44).

It is evident that this is an exceptionally old place of worship but it does not seem likely that the old chapel will ever be found although special individual stones can be seen in the old graveyard.

2. *Teampall Mholuidh*   NB 2006

The Origines map (1851) identifies the site of a chapel as 'St. Malrube's' close to Màraig.

The Old Statistical Account (1794) mentions a chapel dedicated to 'St. Rufus'.

No one is certain of the spot where the chapel was situated.

An Teampall, An Taobh Tuath.

3. *An Teampall, An Taobh Tuath*

The name of Alasdair Crotach — one of the chiefs of MacLeod of Harris, who died in 1547 — is closely linked with the Harris chapels. And it is written that Alasdair Crotach built this chapel: that he built it at 'Nic Capevale', a few years before his death.

The walls and gables of the chapel are still intact, and it is situated in a beautiful spot by the shore, south of Ceapabhal.

The Royal Commission (1928) states, "It is a single chambered oblong structure, measuring 21 feet by 10 inches, with walls about $2\frac{2}{3}$ feet thick." (31).

Above it and to the north, can still be found the well called Tobar an t-Sagairt: there would surely have been priests associated with the chapel.

T.S. Muir (1885) says of this chapel, "Prettily situated on a green mound on the south side of the peninsula of Toe Head, and backed by Bein Chaipabhall, 1200 feet in height, stand the considerable remains of a chapel — in all liklihood one or other of the two spoken of in the 'Origines Parochiales' as having been dedicated to Saints Maelrubha and Luke." (44).

Tùr Mòr Chliamain

4. Tùr Mòr Chliamain NG 046832

This is the best known chapel in the Western Isles, its architecture and design being distinct from the others.

In 1549 Dean Monro wrote, "In the south part of this isle lies a monastery with a steeple, which was founded and built by Macleod of Harris, called Rodel." (86).

This was Alasdair Crotach, who died two years previously and who is buried in a tomb inside the church — the tomb engraving being a renowned and powerful Highland icon.

The chapel was undoubtedly built on the site of a previous cell or church, but it was Alasdair Crotach who built it in its present form.

It was burnt to the ground when the Protestant faith arrived in the 16th century — as were many other churches — and nothing remained of the structure but the walls until they were rebuilt by the innovative Captain Alasdair MacLeod in the 18th century. One hundred years later it was again repaired.

A wealth of visual and oral information surrounds the totality of this chapel, and much of that defines the lives of the people of Harris through the centuries.

The islands are extremely fortunate that such an historic site exists, in order to give us a sense of historic place. (see Lawson, 1991; Macaulay, 1993; Royal Commission, 1928, 32-37).

5. *An Teampall, An Scarp*

This chapel was situated in the graveyard at Scarp, but little now remains of it.

The inhabitants of Scarp called the graveyard, 'An Teampall'.

It was Alasdair Crotach who also built this chapel, as well as St. Clement's and the chapel at Northton.

An 18th century account says, "Allister Crottach built two other beautiful Small Churches dependent on the monastery (St. Clement's) — one at Nic Capevale (Ceapabhal) and one in Scarp — now both in ruins." (see Duncan, 1995, 173).

6. *Eaglais Tarain and Teampall Chè*   NG 031992

The sites of these two buildings are on Taransay.

Martin Martin talks of, "two chapels, one dedicated to St. Tarran, and the other to St. Keith." (123).

The Royal Commission (1928) says, "The stones having been removed, all that remains are two slight mounds within a few yards of the shore to the south-west of the township. Both chapels seem to have been oriented east and west, the mound of the western chapel, St. Keith's, measuring 21 feet in length by 12 feet in breadth, while that of the other, St. Taran's, which lies 38 yards to the east, is 32 feet long by 18 feet broad." (31).

Martin Martin gives an account of an unusual practice which the islanders followed in respect of the two graveyards, associated with both chapels: "There is an ancient tradition among the natives here that a man must not be buried in St. Tarran's, nor a woman in St. Keith's, because otherwise the corpse would be found above the ground the day after it is interred." (123).

Clach an Teampaill (NG 013008) is situated on the island, close to Uidh, but there is no sign of a chapel. (see Lawson, 1997).

7. *Teampall na h-Annaid* NF 975847

The site of this chapel is in the old graveyard on the island of Killegray, above Caolas Sgàire. The Old Statistical Account (1791) states, "In the north end of the island of Calligray, there are faint traces of a very ancient building, called Teampall na h-Annaid... Near this temple is a well of water, at which the worshippers purified themselves, called Tobair na h-Annaid, and the point of land on which it is situated is called Ru na h-Annaid." (82).

The Royal Commission (1928) says, "It lies almost due east and west, and measures 21 feet in length by 12 feet in breadth internally, the mound of the wall being about 3 feet six inches thick. The door seems to have been in the centre of the western gable." (37).

One can also find Annaidean elsewhere: in Swainbost, and in Shader, Barvas; and in the Shiants.

8. *Teampall Easaigh* NF 981866

This chapel was repaired and roofed in 1910 — around the same time as Teampall Mholuidh in Eoropie. Both were repaired by the Episcopalian Church, although that church had no previous links with them.

The Royal Commission (1928) states, "It is single chambered and oblong in plan, measuring 23 by 12 feet." (37).

All Martin Martin said was, "There is an old chapel here, for the use of the natives." (124).

9. *Teampall Mhuire* NF 889869

This one is in the old graveyard at Baile na Cille in Pabbay.

Martin Martin relates, "There are two chappels on this island, one of which is dedicated to the Virgin Mary, the other to St. Moluag." (123).

They are referred to in the ONB as 'Teampall Mhoire' and 'Teampall Beag'. (Inverness, 5-7)

Part of Teampall Mhuire can still be seen, although the east gable has fallen. This was a large building, close to 40 feet long.

An unusual feature of this site is the way ground is shored up against these ruins, maybe because the site was a graveyard.

This is a peaceful, pleasant spot — on a beautiful and attractive island.

10. *Teampall Mholuidh* NF 889870

This one is very close to Teampall Mhuire in Pabbay. It is much smaller, about 13 feet long. The east side is still intact. This one seems to be the older one.

11. *Teampall Mholuidh* NF 913807

This chapel is located on the island of Berneray; in Cladh Mholuidh above the village of Borve.

Morrison (1989) states, "Its walls were standing in 1890 and its roof was formed apparently by stones gradually sloping to form a roof — like the old Irish celtic oratory. The walls were of course vandalised and little of it now appears above ground." (60).

12. *Cill Aiseam* NF 924826

This chapel is on the island of Berneray. The Old Statistical Account (1791) states, "There is a ruin in the island of Berneray, called, in the vitiated pronounciation of the people, Cill Aisaim..." (84).

The Royal Commission (1928) states, "No trace of the foundations of the church indicated by the name is now visible." (38).

Martin Martin refers to this chapel as 'St. Asaph's', and he mentions that there is an 8 foot high standing stone close to it.

Morrison 1989 wrote, "St. Asaph... had a church dedicated to him in Berneray. Its sanctuary was marked by crosses in the middle ages... Near the site of the temple is a stone over 8 feet broad which has now fallen, but which was erect at the time Martin Martin visited the site..." (8).

North Uist

1. Eilean an Teampaill   NF 904707

This is a small island about two miles west of Lochmaddy: it is accessible at low tide. There is some kind of site there, but no certainty of there having been a chapel, and no knowledge of a name.

North of this, in Lochportain there are three names — 'Loch an t-Sagairt', 'Cnoc Mòr an t-Sagairt' and 'Cnoc Beag an t-Sagairt' — but there is no sign of a chapel.

2. Teampall Chaluim Chille   NF 873765

This site is in Clachan Shannda and by all accounts is very old.

Origines (1851) says, "Undoubtedly one of the two parish churches of North Uist mentioned by Dean Monro in 1549" (376). It is shown on Timothy Pont's map of 1600 as 'Kilchalmkil'. (Blaeu, 1654).

T.S. Muir (1861) wrote, "The west end of the chapel is standing, the rest of it greatly reduced, and partly buried under a huge sand-heap.' (225). Nowadays only the lower structure of the wall is visible in the east side of the graveyard: the graveyard is still in use. An extremely ancient site.

Half a mile to the south-east of the chapel there is a large stone (Martin Martin: "... about 8 feet high at Downrossel which the natives call a cross.") which has a number of names: 'Clach an t-Sagairt', 'Clach na h-Ulaidh', and 'Crois Adhamhnain' (St. Adamnan).

Tobar Chaluim Chille is situated a mile south of the chapel.

About 100 yards north of the chapel site there is a place called 'Druim na Croise'. MacRury (1950) states, "North of St. Columba Chapel on the Hornish end of 'Druim na Croise' there was a more ancient chapel dedicated to a St. Goulba." (14). Beveridge (1911) also mentions it.

3. *Cladh Bhoraraigh*   NF 855804

Although no sign can be seen of a chapel site on Boreray, 'Cladh nam Manach' can be seen on the OS map. Martin Martin wrote, "The Burial place near the Houses, is called the Monks-Field, for all the Monks that dyed in the Islands that lye Northward from Egg, were buried in this little Plot." (69).

4. *An Teampall, Orasaigh*   NF 847757

Although a site was found on Orasaigh some years ago, no one is entirely sure that it was a chapel site.

The site is called 'Pàirce an Teampaill'.

5. *Sgeilear, Sollas* NF 806757

The old Sgeilear graveyard is situated here, but there is no sign of a chapel ruin nor is there a chapel name now associated with it. MacCulloch (1824) gives the following account, "... an ancient chapel situated in the north west-angle of the island." The east gable was still standing at that time, and was situated on a sand bank. Beveridge (1911) says, "The circumstantial account given by that writer (MacCulloch) cannot apply to any other locality than Skellor." (299).

6. *Ard a' Mhorain* NF 837787

There is no evidence of the location of a chapel or any name associated with a chapel in the old graveyard at Ard a' Mhorain. But Tobar an t-Sagairt is situated above the shore about 200 yards west of the graveyard, and there is a cross carved out in the rock above it.

7. *Teampall Mhuire* NF 786764

This is on Vallay Island, south of the old graveyard.

It is referred to by Martin Martin as, "It (Vallay) hath Three Chappels, One dedicated to St. Ulton, and another to the Virgin Mary." (67).

The Royal Commission (1928) states, "Only portions of the foundations remain... These foundations are confined to what seems to have been a chancel, about 9 or 10 feet square. The walling is 3 feet thick. A depression in the ground probably indicates the lines of a nave some three feet wider than the chancel." (51).

There were also two crosses in the vicinity. Beveridge found one of them in 1904, used as a lintel on the entrance to a burial aisle there. In 1885 T.S. Muir saw the other cross standing in the graveyard. Martin Martin had mentioned them both.

According to oral tradition there was once a nunnery on this island.

8. *Teampall Ultain* NF 786763

Martin Martin mentions this chapel located on Vallay Island, although there is now no sign of it. It is thought to have been close to Teampall Mhoire. It is not mentioned in oral tradition or on the early maps. Chapels dedicated to St. Ultan are not at all common in Scotland.

9. Teampall Orain NF 773771

This chapel is in Orasaigh, at the north west point of Vallay Island.

The Royal Commission (1928) states, "On the west side of the peninsula of Oronsay are the foundations of a rectangular building lying east and west. The walls are dry built and about 4 feet thick, while the whole structure measures 24 by 17 feet internally." (50).

Beveridge (1911) states, "Adjoining the south side of this Teampall is some appearance of a semi-circular enclosure." (297).

10. Cille Pheadair NF 726744

There is no sign now of this chapel, but it is known that it was located on the south side of a small hillock across from Balelone. It could be the one located on the John Speed map (1610) and referred to there as 'St. Patricius'.

Beveridge actually places it, "We are assured upon excellent authority that its burial ground has been recently exposed in course of ploughing the field. Its former site is indicated as a grassy plateau immediately to the south of Kilphedar Cross which now stands at the summit of the knoll, raised upon a modern square pedestal $6\frac{1}{2}$ feet high. This cross was originally within the graveyard, having been removed to its present position by Dr. Alexander MacLeod (An Sgoilear Bàn) of Balelone about 1930-1840." (296).

11. *Teampall Chliamain* NF 711728

This chapel site is situated in the old graveyard north of Tigharry.

On Blaeu's map (1654) and in Origines (1851) it is called 'Kilchalma' and 'Kilchalman', as if it were dedicated to St. Columba.

The ONB states, "It was dedicated to St. Clement and was a christening chapel & place of worship immediately preceeding Kilmuir (the present parish church). (Inverness, 5-7).

The Royal Commission (1928) says, "The foundations of St. Clement's Chapel are still discernable. The building has been oblong, lying almost east and west, and measuring about 14 feet 6 inches in length and about 10 feet 9 inches in breadth internally. The door has been in the western gable." (50).

12. Cill Mhuire

This chapel was located in the graveyard south of Hogarry.

In Monro's time (1549) both this one and Teampall Chaluim Chille were the two parish churches in North Uist.

Oral tradition had it that the builders of this chapel were visited beforehand by a voice which instructed them: "Avoid Hough and Hosta, and build Cill Mhuire in Colasaidh." (The surrounding area is still called Colasaidh)

There is no evidence nowadays of this chapel but it is known that it was in the graveyard.

On Aird an Rùnaire, west of Cill Mhuire, there are two interesting names. 'Cladh Chòthain' is referred to as having been located on the east side of Aird an Rùnaire, but no site has as yet been found. There are a number of chapels dedicated to Còthan in the Highlands.

And 'Eilean Trostain' is at the north side of Aird an Rùnaire: Trostan was closely linked to St. Columba.

13. Teampall Chrìosd
NF 783613

This chapel was in the graveyard at Baleshare and part of the west wall is still visible.

The Royal Commission (1928) states, "The foundations of the church, oblong on plan, are traceable with difficulty, but the building seems to have been about 42 feet long and about 12 feet broad internally, possibly with a divisional wall about 18 feet from the west end. It is oriented east by north and west by south...

"About 130 yards to the north-north-west is a conspicuous grassy ridge, known as Crois Mhor, while to the east is Creag Thormaidh, both supposed to be sanctuary limits." (49).

The local people are of the opinion that this is one of the churches built by Amie NicRuaraidh in Uist in the 14th century.

Tradition has it that there is a place called 'Baile na Cille,' in Iolaraigh, close to Teampall Chrìosd. (see Beveridge, 1911, 290).

Teampall na Trianaid

14. Teampall na Trianaid

This is one of the large well known island chapels, and a lot has been written about it.

Apparently a small chapel occupied the site in early times, although it did not enjoy the status of a parish church as did Teampall Mhuire in Cille Mhuire, and Teampall Chaluim Chille in Sannda. Teampall na Trianaid was re-built at least twice, and hardly anything remains of the original building.

According to tradition the chapel was built (or re-built) by Beathag, daughter of Somhairle, early in the 13th century, and it was repaired again by Amie NicRuairidh 150 years after that.

Although it has deteriorated, a substantial part of the walls still remain, which ensures that people are more aware of it than they are of any other old chapels in North Uist. The chapel housed large sculptured stones at one time, similar to those in Tùr Chliamain in Harris, but they are not there now.

This chapel has a lot of history attached to it: it was a university for priests, taught by a well known family of professors — the MacVicars; it was burnt to the ground by Uisdean MacGilleasbaig Clèireach — one of the MacDonalds of Sleat — after the Reformation in the 16th century.

It is said that the acclaimed philosopher, Duns Scotus, was a student at this chapel. Tradition has it that it was used as a university up to the 17th century. (see Royal Commission, 1928; Beveridge, 1911; MacDonald, 1972).

15. *Teampall Clann Mhic a' Phiocair*   NF 816603
This building is attached to Teampall na Trianaid.

The Royal Commission (1928) states, "... a second structure, apparently a house and not a chapel, though known as Teampall MacVicar... The house is evidently subsequent (to the Teampall) and possibly dates from later in the 16th century." (48).

16. *Heisgeir nan Cailleach*   NF 645623
At the east side there is an old graveyard known as 'Cladh na Bleide' and about which Beveridge (1911) wrote, "It has almost certainly associated with a former chapel, of which no tradition seems now to remain although a slight wall is visible at the west base of a sand-hill." (291).

Tradition tells of a large monastery and of a large nunnery on Heisgeir.

MacRury (1950) says, "Heisker... is a place which had a long connection with Iona; it could boast a nunnery which continued to function till the time of the Reformation. A lighthouse now casts its warning beam over Eilean nam Manach, where, in days that are no more, nuns paid their devotions in the dim light of a seal-oil lamp... Up to about sixty years ago the site of the nunnery could be traced in the Ceann-an-Iar." (13).

17. Teampall Mhìcheil   NF 882548

This chapel is on the island of Grimsay in a place called Na Ceallan. It is situated on Rubha Mhìcheil with Eileanan an Teampaill some distance away.

It is confirmed that Amie NicRuairaidh built the chapel in the 14th century — as she built Teampall Chriosd in Baile Sear, and had repaired Teampall na Trianaid.

F.W. Thomas (1871) says, "the east wall being quite gone, and the south side, in which was the door, is but 3 feet high. There is 9 feet of the west wall left." (244).

Beveridge visited in 1905: "The north wall showed recent damage and was nowhere more than 3 feet high, without any appearance of the two windows mentioned by Captain Thomas." (1911, 279).

The Royal Commission (1928) states, "It is an oblong structure of stone and lime, oriented, and measuring internally 23 feet 2 inches in length by 13 feet 8 inches in breadth. The walls... are reduced to a height of about $1\frac{1}{2}$ feet, except the western gable, which stands 8 feet high, and a small part of the south wall, which is 3 feet in height on the inside." (47).

Alexander Carmichael informs us that he found the site of another chapel in a small graveyard about 150 yards north of Teampall Mhìcheil.

18. *Teampall Rònaigh*   NF 885572

The island of Rona lies to the east of the island of Grimsay. On the north west side of the island one finds names such as Rubha an t-Sagairt and Beinn an t-Sagairt. There is also a spot called Cnoc nan Gall.

This ties in with what Martin Martin says, "a little Chappel in the Island of Rona, called the Lowlanders Chappel, because seamen who dye in time of Fishing, are buried in that place." (279).

Benbecula

1. Teampall Chaluim Chille   NF 782549

This chapel is in Balivanich; it is on raised ground, surrounded by bog where Loch Chaluim Chille once was. At one time it was accessible by a path and it was surrounded by four crosses. Tobar Chaluim Chille is about 200 yards south west of the chapel.

A large proportion of the walls is still intact, but little information on it is available.

It is marked on Timothy Pont's map of approximately 1600 as 'Kilcholambkil'.

The Royal Commission (1928) states, "The church has been oblong on plan, and, by a later extension, two-chambered, but the extent of the nave cannot definitely be ascertained, the side walls being breached... The total internal dimensions are $47\frac{1}{2}$ feet from east to west by $14\frac{1}{2}$ feet; the gables are $3\frac{1}{2}$ feet thick, the eastern is reduced to the foundations, while the western remains to the height of the entrance lintel. The lateral walls, breached in places, stand on an average 8 feet above the present ground level." (99).

Origines (1851) says the following, "At Baillvanich (monks' town) on the north west coast on a small island in a lake are remains said to be those of a monastery, but probably the remains of a chapel belonging to the monks of Iona." (370).

Teampall Chaluim Chille

And T.S. Muir (1861) says, " A few yards off it, in a westerly direction, are the foundations of another oblong building, which was probably another chapel." (226).

Tradition tells us of how Teampall Chaluim Chille was built. St. Taran came ashore in the little bay in Balivanich which is called Callegeo. He wanted to build a chapel there, on Cnoc Feannaig, but the angels made him change the location to where it now is. The saint was also thirsty — he prayed and the lovely well, known as An Gàmhnach, over to the side of Ruaidhebhal opened up. (see Carmichael, 1900, 80-83).

2. *Teampall Mhuire* NF 765537

This chapel is in Nunton, in the old graveyard, Cille Mhuire. There is not much historical information available, apart from what visiting writers have written.

Martin Martin relates, "There is also some small Chappels here, one of them at Bael-nin-Killach." (150).

The Royal Commission (1928) says, "Within a graveyard at Nunton is the roofless shell of a small church, oblong on plan, built of rublle in mortar. It measures $24\frac{1}{2}$ feet by $15\frac{1}{2}$ feet over walls $2\frac{1}{2}$ feet thick... The ruin is in fair condition, but the ground has silted up considerably." (99).

There is no sign at all of the building once occupied by nuns after which the place is named. According to the New Statistical Account, "In the island of Benbecula there was a nunnery on the farm called Nuntown. The building was taken down and the stones used in the building of Clanranald's mansion and office-houses." (188).

T.S. Muir (1861) has given the following information, "Nuntown, pleasantly situated about a couple of miles southward of Baile-manaich was the site of a nunnery, the remains of which were removed within the last forty of fifty years to build a 'mansion' for the last highland proprietor. In the adjacent burying-ground of Kilmuir, however, are preserved nearly entire the shell of the church of St. Mary." (226-227).

3. Griminis   NF 802518

It was said that there was a meeting-house here but that its stones were used to build an Established Church close by.

There is no information available about the original building.

4. Teampall Bhuirgh   NF 769503

This building has virtually disappeared into the machair land.

The Royal Commission (1928) says, "The ruined Teampull Bhuirgh, almost covered with blown sand, which reaches the top of the walls on the outside and partly fills the interior... It has been about 46 feet in length, and about 17 feet 10 inches in breadth internally. The gables have disappeared... and the inner face of the masonry has withered away." (100).

South Uist

1. Cill Amhlaigh NF 755463

The old graveyard of Kilaulay is near the village of that name west of Ardkenneth Church in Iochdar. The graveyard is marked on the Ordnance Survey map as, 'Burial Ground disused'. It was apparently in this graveyard that the meeting house called Cill Amhlaigh was situated. Donald John MacDonald (1981) wrote, "The small local churches were called meeting houses. This was before the Reformation." (12).

'Kileulay' is shown on Timothy Pont's map of Uist about 1600. (Blaeu, 1654).

West of 'Kileulay' on Pont's map, is 'Kilehainie': could there have been a meeting house there with a name like Cill Choinnich? And was it from there that the name Aird Choinnich came from?

2. *Cille Bhanain*

Loch Cille Bhanain lies west of Gerinish but there is no sign of the site of the actual cell. T.S. Muir (1861) mentions that there was once an old graveyard here although it is not now much in evidence. (227). It is named on the OS map as 'Chapel in ruins'.

Timothy Pont (1600) marks it on his map as 'Kiluanen'. (Blaeu, 1654). Martin Martin refers to it as 'St. Bannan'. (155).

The Royal Commission (1928) says, "It is oblong on plan, and is built almost due north and south. It measures some 54 feet in length, and 23 feet in breadth externally... It is in danger of collapsing in different places... The structure has been built partly on the site of a dun." (120).

Hoghmòr

3. Hoghmòr

This is one of the best known and interesting sites in the whole of the Western Isles — it comprises not just one site, but a number. According to Monro (1549) both this one and Teampall Chille Pheadair were the two parish churches in South Uist.

Martin Martin says, "The churches here are St. Columba and St. Mary's in Hogh-more, the most centrical place in the island." (155).

T.S. Muir gives a detailed account of 5 separate buildings which comprise Hoghmòr although he does not name them all. The largest one is 60 feet long and he writes of it: "This was probably the ecclesia matrix of South Uist, and that which is mentioned by Martin as under the dedication of St. Mary." (228).

When T.S. Muir returned after forty years he found the situation as follows: "Howmore at my first visit had remains of five churches and chapels, all standing close by one another. One of the number I now found had been removed during the late operation of inclosing the burial-ground... The missing one was a very characteristic building, the smallest of the group, with a very narrow rectangular window and a short sloping doorway in the east end. Externally it measured only 17 $\frac{1}{2}$ feet in length." (280). This one was to the south of the large one furthest west; this was 'Caibeal nan Sagairt'.

Caibeal Chlann 'ic Ailein was at the north-east end of the graveyard.

The OS names three of the chapels: An Teampall Mòr; Caibeal nan Sagairt; and Caibeal Dhiarmaid.

Donald John MacDonald (1981) writes about Hoghmòr: "There were two churches in the parish of Howmore, St. Mary's church and St. Columba's. The remains of these two churches can be seen to the present day, and even the end wall of one of them is still standing... the old graveyard at Hoghmòr was the burial place of the Clanranalds, the area known as Caibeal Chlann 'ic Ailein." (12).

It was from here that the Clanranald stone was taken some years ago; it is now in the museum at Kildonan School.

MacDonald also added: "Added to the two large churches in Howmore, there was apparently an education college there, similar to Càirinis in North Uist, and the college and the churches, as well as St. Peter's church came under the authority of Iona." (12).

4. *Cill Aird Mhìcheil* NF 7333

Nothing remains of this site, but it was apparently situated in the old graveyard out at Aird Mhìcheil.

Martin Martin refers to it as 'St. Michael'. (155).

5. *Clachan a' Chumhaing* NF 7432

There is nothing left of this meeting house except the name.

Origines (1851) maps it as 'Clachan Cuay'. Donald John MacDonald (1981) calls it 'Clachan a' Chumhaing'.

6. *Cill Donnain* NF 731282

The OS map names this as 'Cill Donnain burial ground (disused)' on a point at the northwest end of Kildonan. It seems that the cell was located here although there is no evidence to that effect now.

'Kildonan ' is mentioned in a paper in 1498 describing how King James IV was giving away land in South Uist. (Origines, 1851, 366).

The cell is named on Timothy Pont's map (1600) as 'Kildonan'. (Blaeu, 1654). Martin Martin refers to it as 'St. Donann'.

The Royal Commission (1928) states, "On a northerly projecting promontary on the west side of the northern half of Loch Kildonan is the site of Cill Donnain, but no trace of any building is now visible." (120).

7. *Circeadal* NF 7927

All that is left of this chapel is the name, meaning the Dale of the Church. Origines (1851) calls it 'Kirkdale', and Donald John MacDonald (1981) mentions that one of the small meeting houses is "in Circedal to the south side of Loch Aoineirt." (13).

8. *Cille Pheadair* NF 735205

Kilpheder was the parish church for the south end of South Uist, as Howmore was the parish church in the north end. Dean Monro (1549) says, "The rest of the Ile callit Peiteris parochin, the parochin of Howf, and the mane land of the mid cuntrey callit Machermeanache." (76).

Although there is not much in evidence of it nowadays, it would seem that this was at one time a large and important chapel. It is referred to as early as the beginning of the 14th century, "In 1309 King Robert the Bruce granted... land in the parish of Kilpedire Blisen." (Origines, 1851, 366).

On Timothy Pont's map of Uist circa 1600, the church of 'Kilphedre' is depicted as being even larger than Hoghmòr. (Blaeu, 1654).

'Cladh Pheadair' is placed on the OS map half way between Loch na Liana Mòire and the shore. And the Royal Commission states, "About $\frac{1}{4}$ mile north of Loch a' Ghearraidh Dhubh, south-west of Daliburgh on the summit of a sand-hill, is Cladh Pheadair. No trace of the burial ground is now visible." (120).

9. *Teampall, Baghasdal*   NF 7317

There is no certainty at present about the location of this chapel.

The ONB states, "A burial ground 1 mile south of North Boisdale and 1 mile north east of South Boisdale and is the supposed site of a chapel." (Inverness, 1878, 92).

10. Cill Choinnich

NF 796200

This one is on the OS map as 'Chapel & Cladh Choinnich (site of)'. The ONB says, "It is traditionally known that there once stood a chapel and a burying ground... But there is none now living who can point out with certainty the exact spot." (Inverness, 1878, 72).

The hill which is nowadays known as Beinn Ruigh Choinnich, east of the village of Lochboisdale, is referred to as 'Bin Kilohainie' by Timothy Pont (1600) — although the chapel itself is not on the Pont map. Neither Martin Martin nor Origines (1851) makes reference to it.

11. Cille Bhrìghde

NF 757141

This site was located in the village of Kilbride, at the south end of the island. It is on Timothy Pont's map (1600) as 'Kilvrid'. It is on the OS map as, 'Site of Cille Bhride (Burial ground)'.

MacDonald (1981) mentions that there was a little church at Kilbride.

The Royal Commission (1928) says, "In the old burying ground at Kilbride is the site of the ancient church of the same name, but all traces of it have been swept away." (120).

There is no information currently available on the following:

1. Martin Martin makes reference to 'St. Jeremy's Chapel' in South Uist.

2. Origines (1851) says, "The oldest men, says a writer of the seventeenth century, report this ile to be much empayred and destroyed be the sands ovirblowing and burieing habitable lands, and the sea hath followed and made the loss irreperable. There are destroyed the tounes and paroch churches of Kilmarchirmor and Kilpetil, and the church of Kilmonie is now called Kilpetil, that is, the church of the muir, for so it lay of old nearest the muirs, but now the sea and the sands have approached it. There be sum remaynes of the destroyed churches yit to be seen at low tydes or ebbing water." (368).

3. Origines (1851) maps a church to the east of Kildonan called 'Clachan of Branagh'. We have no information as to whether this linked up with Cladh Ard an Dugain which is marked on the OS map on a headland to the west of Loch Grianabreic in Airigh-Mhuilinn.

Cille Bharra

Barra

1. *Cille Bharra*NF 705074

This is a particularly important church.

Dean Monro (1549) refers to Barra as being, " with ane paroche kirke named Kilbarr." Timothy Pont (1600) maps it as 'Kilbarra'.

Martin Martin (1695) states, "The church in this island is called Kilbarr, i.e., St. Barr's Church. There is a little chapel by it... The natives have St. Barr's wooden image standing on the alter, covered with linen in form of a shirt... (158).

"All the inhabitants observe the anniversary of St. Barr, being the 27th of September; it is performed riding on horseback, and the solemnity is concluded by three turns round St. Barr's Church. (163).

"They have likewise a general calvalcade on St. Michael's Day, in Kilbar village, and do then also take a turn round their church. Every family, as soon as the solemnity is ended, is accustomed to bake St. Michael's cake... and all strangers, together with those of the family, must eat the bread that night." (164).

The Royal Commission (1928) says, "the remains of a church and two dedicated chapels, grouped with the Church to the west and the chapels lying eastward and to either side... The church, which was dedicated to St. Barr, measures 38 feet by $13\frac{1}{4}$ feet within walls averaging $2\frac{1}{2}$ feet thick. The gables are reduced almost to the ground level, but the side walls stand to a height of 7 or 8 feet... The northern chapel measures 26 feet by 9 ¾ feet... The third chapel measures 14 ½ feet by 8 ¼ feet." (123-124).

The 'northern chapel' — or Caibeal Mhuire — was re-roofed a few years ago, and ancient sculptured stones are retained there. It was here that the only runic stone ever to be seen in the Western Isles was found; it is now in the National Museum in Edinburgh.

To the east of Cille Bharra graveyard can be found the famous well called Tobar Bharra — an exquisite well with its sandy bottom. (see J.L. Campbell, 1936; Macquarrie, 1989).

2. *Cill Bhrianain* NF 647017

The lower remains of this chapel are in the village of Borve along the shoreline.

The Royal Commission (1928) says, "In a burying ground on the south side of the low-lying peninsula terminating in Borve Point, just above the sea-shore, is a fragment of an old church, St. Brendan's Chapel, built of stone and lime... Only a small portion of a gable remains, standing about 3 feet in height, with part of the northern jamb of a door in position." (125).

Some of the written accounts refer to 'Cille Mhìcheil' as having been the name of this chapel. The Statistical Account (1794) says, "In Kilbar are two churches, built by the monks, belonging to Icolumkill; another at Borve, dedicated to St. Michael." (335).

T.S. Muir's account of the site (1885) is as follows, "It has been a building of very moderate size, consisting of a chancel and nave, respectively only 7 feet 10 inches and 23 feet in length, inside... I may mention, as perhaps worth recording, that the only other ecclesiastical building I have fallen in with in the Long Island in which the chancel and the nave are constructively separated, is the almost similarly proportioned church of St. John Baptist, at Bragar, on the west side of Lewis." (283).

The Bishop's Isles

To the south of Barra lie the Bishop's Isles; Dean Monro (1549) identifies nine islands and tells that each one of them had a chapel — Lingay; Gigarun; Berneray; Megaly (Mingulay); Pabay; Fladay; Scarpnamut (Muldonaich); Sanderay; Watersay. Monro says, "All thir nine Iles forsaid had a Chapell in every Ile." (72-73).

3. Cille Bhrianain   NL 664957

This chapel is on the east side of Vatersay, in Uineasain. It is also called, 'Caibeal Moire nan Ceann'. The story is told of Moire having been a wild woman, beheading anyone who was not to her liking. She was from the Isle of Coll, and she wished to be buried in full view of that island. The funeral procession became weary of carrying her and they buried her in Uineasain although Maoldònaich is between her resting place and Coll.

The Royal Commission (1928) comments, "... an old burying ground containing the foundations of an old church of stone and lime... The building has been oblong and oriented east-north-east and west-south-west. It has been about 37 feet long and 16 feet 6 inches broad externally." (137).

4. Cille Bhrìghde   NL 651920

This chapel was situated on Sandray.

The Royal Commission (1928) says, "In an old burying ground above the shore to the south-east of Bagh Ban, near the north-east corner of Sandray, are faint traces of the ancient chapel of Cille Bhride. The larger part of the site is occupied by a sheep fank, but a corner of its foundations built of stone and lime can be detected." (137).

The chapel has now completely been engulfed by sand.

5. Cill, Pabaigh   NL 607874

The name of this island— and every other island with the same name — means a place where a monk resided at one time. And Monro says that there was a chapel on this island as was on all the others round about.

The Royal Commission (1928) says, "On what is now a mound some 10 feet high, on the south western border of the sandy slope running up from Bagh Ban on the eastern shore of Pabbay, about 150 yards from the high-water mark, are the indistinct foundations of an oblong church of stone and lime measuring 31 feet in length and 14 feet in breadth externally, and oriented slightly north of west and south of east." (126).

It is not easy to find this site; the sand has engulfed it over the years.

The singular Pictish stone of the Western Isles was found here during this present century, and other stone slabs with crosses on them were also found.

6. *Cill Chaluim Chille*   NL 565833

This chapel was located on Mingulay.

The Royal Commission (1928) says, "No traces of St. Columba's Chapel are to be seen. It stood above the shore at the north-west corner of Mingulay Bay, a sandy bay on the east side of the island." (137).

Buxton (1995) tells that, "The officers of the Ordnance Survey were informed in 1878 of the traditional site of a chapel, dedicated to St. Columba, with graveyard attached. This was the knoll, occupied by the graveyard, next to the stream in the village, and the corner of a building is now visible on the knoll... Graveyards on all four of the other main islands south of Barra (Bhatarsaigh, Sanndaigh, Pabaigh agus Beàrnaraigh) are similarly the traditional sites of chapels, though only on Mingulay are there visible remains." (31).

7. Cill, Beàrnaraigh   NL 567803

This chapel was located on the Isle of Berneray, but the name is not now known.

The Royal Commission (1928) says, "Near MacLean's Point some 350 yards east by south of the landing jetty on the island of Bernera and about 50 yards from the shore in an old burying ground is the sire of a church, all traces of which have disappeared." (137).

If anything is left of the building, it has been engulfed by sand long ago.

A stone slab with an engraving of a cross was found near at hand: it was at least 1,000 years old.

At the end of his journey through the islands, T.S. Muir arrived at Bernera on the 15th of July 1866. Although he did not find any signs of the old graveyard and the chapel, he rested, "Bernera — Here, after innumerable jumblings by land and sea, I am — thanks for it! — at the end of my journey, and taking a few days' rest in the lighthouse." (1885, 254). What a fortunate man.

Books

John Barber, 1987, Innsegall: The Western Isles. John Donald.

Erskine Beveridge, 1911, North Uist.

Ben Buxton, 1995, Mingulay. Birlinn.

John Lorne Campbell et al, 1936, The Book of Barra. Routledge.

Alexander Carmichael, 1972, Carmina Gadelica. Scottish Academic Press.

Ian B. Cowan, 1967, The Parishes of Medieval Scotland. Scottish Record Society.

Frank Fraser Darling, 1939, A Naturalist on Rona. Oxford.

Angus Duncan, 1995, Hebridean Island. Memories of Scarp. Tuckwell Press.

James Hogg, 1888, A Tour in the Highlands in 1803. Gardner.

Bill Lawson, 1991, St. Columba's Church at Aignish; 1991, St. Clements Church at Rodel; 1993, The Teampull at Northton and The Church at Scarista; 1993, St. Kilda and its Church; 1994, The Temple on the Isle of Pabbay; 1997, The Isle of Taransay. Bill Lawson Publications.

John Macaulay, 1993, Silent Tower. Pentland.

Murdo MacAulay, c1984, Aspects of the Religious History of Lewis.

Kenneth MacAulay, 1764, The History of St. Kilda. James Thin.

John McCulloch, 1824, The Highlands & Western Isles of Scotland. Longman.

Dr. MacDonald of Gisla, 1967, Tales and Traditions of the Lews. Mrs MacDonald.

Donald Macdonald, 1978, Lewis; A History of the Island. Gordon Wright.

Dòmhnall Iain MacDhòmhnaill, 1981, Uibhist a Deas. Acair.

Norman Macdonald, 1972, Trinity Temple, North Uist.

W.C. MacKenzie, 1903, The History of the Outer Hebrides; 1932, The Western Isles. Gardner.

Finlay Macleod (ed), 1989, Togail Tir. Acair/An Lanntair.

Alan Macquarrie, 1989, Cille Bharra. Grant Books.

Ewen MacRury, 1950, A Hebridean Parish. Northern Chronicle Office.

Martin Martin, 1934, A Voyage to St. Kilda; A Description of the Western Isles of Scotland. Eneas Mackay.

Dean Monro, 1549, Western Isles of Scotland.

(ed. R.W. Munro, 1961, Oliver and Boyd).

Alick Morrison, 1989, The Island of Berneray and its History.

T.S. Muir, 1861, Characteristics of Old Church Architecture; 1885, Ecclesiological Notes on Some of the Islands of Scotland. David Douglas.

Origines Parochiales Scotiae, 1851. Lizars.

Ordnance Survey Original Object Name Books (ONB).

D.D.C. Pochin Mould, 1953, West Over Sea. Oliver & Boyd.

Michael Robson, 1991, Rona; The Distant Island. Acair.

Royal Commission, 1928, Ancient and Historical Monuments of Scotland: The Outer Hebrides, Skye and the Small Isles. HMSO.

Notes

Notes